Hot Chefs

favourite recipes from eight of Britain's top chefs

BBC

Published 1993 by Broadcasting Support
Services to accompany **Hot Chefs** (a
Kershaw Production Associates production
for BBC in the Midlands), first shown on
BBC1 June–July 1993.

Recipes checked and compiled by:
  Valerie Barrett
Booklet design:
  Broadcasting Support Services
Cover illustration:
  Blake Laurent Design Associates
Food photography: David Palmer
Printed by: Haynes Cannon
Distributed by:
  Broadcasting Support Services

Broadcasting Support Services is an
educational charity, which runs helplines
and provides follow-up services for viewers
and listeners.

For further copies, please send a cheque or
postal order for £2.75 (payable to BSS) to:

Hot Chefs
PO Box 7
London W3 6XJ

ISBN: 0–906965–67–5

Dear Viewer,

Although I suppose I should address you now as 'Dear Reader' since you have taken your courage in your hands and are about to attempt some (dare I say all?) of the 44 recipes of **Hot Chefs 1993**!

I think your first challenge is going to be which recipe you start with. We've got everything here; from breakfast to dinner, from Japanese to Olde English, not forgetting fish, fowl, fancy, plain, sweet, savoury, hot, cold, roasted, toasted, basted, sliced and diced! Well, I think you could start just about anywhere and I know that if I was sitting down at your table I would enjoy every mouthful.

But before you disappear into the kitchen I'd like to take a moment to thank all the chefs who have allowed us to reprint their recipes from the series. All of them have studied and worked for years to perfect their craft and I am very grateful to them for allowing us to reveal their secrets.

One thing I particularly noticed watching all the chefs at work is that 'a pinch of this' and 'a dash of that' really is the language of the professional chef. I think that watching them work is as close to watching real magic as you can get. But for the purpose of this book I have had all the recipes checked out and our home economists have given precise measures wherever necessary. However, I'm sure you will all develop your own variations.

In this series we added an extra dimension to each programme when I was allowed to roam the country in search of real food fanatics: not just chefs, but market traders, spice importers, Japanese restaurant owners, butlers, farmers and waiters. Their knowledge was exhaustive and their welcome always friendly, but above all their enthusiasm for food was wonderfully infectious. My thanks to them all. I came away a wiser, if hungrier, man.

Finally a last word of thanks to my crew at Pebble Mill – a Scotch broth of leftovers if ever there was one. Before we started filming their idea of a square meal was anything between two slices of white bread. Now they all want foie gras and Parma ham in their chip butties. Thanks guys!

But I know you, dear reader, have a more discerning palate. So on with your aprons, sharpen your knives and turn the pages. And you too will soon be a 'Hot Chef'.

Good luck – and *bon appétit*!

Contents

Hot Chefs

John Burton-Race

Recreation: 'very little'. Overall this is not a career recommended for those given to resting on laurels – or resting at all, for that matter – and it's not surprising that a chef as successful as John Burton-Race may have to leave philatelic pursuits for another life. He started as an apprentice at the Wessex Hotel in Winchester, gradually working his way up through a series of jobs and restaurants, including Le Manoir aux Quat' Saisons, where Clive Fretwell is now chef (see page 15). He has been at his restaurant L'Ortolan, in Shinfield, near Reading, since 1986.

Filet d'Agneau en Croute de Sel

Serves 4

2.3 kg (5 lb) best end of lamb
oil for frying
1 onion, chopped
1 stick celery, chopped
1 carrot, chopped
2 shallots, chopped
about 2 litres (3 $^1/_2$ pints) chicken stock
2 cloves garlic
1 sprig rosemary, crushed
$^1/_2$ bay leaf
1 sprig thyme
125 g (4 oz) mushrooms, chopped

Salt crust
250 g (9 oz) plain flour
250 g (9 oz) coarse sea salt
1 teaspoon chopped rosemary
1 teaspoon chopped thyme
1 whole egg
1 egg yolk
water to mix

Persillage
200 g (7 oz) white breadcrumbs
2 cloves garlic, crushed and chopped
1 teaspoon chopped thyme
1 teaspoon chopped rosemary
60 g (2 oz) flat parsley, very finely chopped
about 2 – 3 teaspoons olive oil
salt and pepper
Dijon mustard

Garnish
10 cloves garlic, left in their skins
20 small shallots, peeled
water
1 teaspoon lemon juice
pinch sugar
salt and pepper
60 g (2 oz) butter

To glaze
beaten egg

/cont.

• Remove the lamb fillets from the best ends and trim off all the fat and sinew. You can ask the butcher to do this for you but ask him to give you the bones and trimmings as well. Heat a little oil in a roasting pan. Put the bones and trimmings in the pan and roast in a hot oven at 200°C (400°F), gas mark 6, for 30 – 40 minutes until golden brown. Turn the bones over occasionally.

• Heat a little oil in a pan and brown the onion, celery, carrot and shallots. Remove and drain. Put the browned lamb bones into a large pan. Pour in the chicken stock. Add the browned vegetables together with the garlic, rosemary, bay leaf, thyme and mushrooms. Bring to the boil and simmer for one hour.

• To make the salt crust, put the flour and salt into a bowl. Add the herbs and mix well together. Add the egg and egg yolk and mix to a pliable dough with a little water. Knead until smooth. Cover with a cloth or clingfilm and leave to rest.

• To make the persillage, put the breadcrumbs, garlic and herbs into a bowl. Add the olive oil a little at a time until a moist, crumbly mixture is obtained. Season.

• Cut each lamb fillet in half so there are four pieces. Season the fillets with pepper only. Heat a little oil in a pan and seal them well on all sides and at the ends. It is important to seal them all over so they do not bleed into the crust. Spread a little Dijon mustard on the lamb pieces and roll in the persillage. Allow to cool completely.

• To make the garnish, blanch the cloves of garlic three times, making sure the third time that the garlic is tender. Put to one side. Put the shallots in a pan with just enough water to cover. Add the lemon juice, sugar, seasoning and butter. Simmer gently until shallots are tender and there is no liquid remaining, just a light buttery glaze.

• Roll out a quarter of the salt crust making it large enough to enclose one piece of lamb. Place the fillet on top and carefully wrap the crust round the lamb, taking care not to leave any cracks or holes. Turn the parcel over leaving the join underneath and put on a baking sheet. Brush with beaten egg.

• Strain the stock and skim off any fat. Put into a pan and bring to the boil. Reduce rapidly by boiling to just under 300 ml (1/2 pint).

• Cook the lamb in a pre-heated oven at 230°C (450°F), gas mark 8, for 9 minutes. Remove from oven and allow to rest for a minute.

• To serve, break open and discard the crust. Slice the lamb and arrange on plates together with the garlic and shallots. Pour over the hot lamb stock and serve.

Hot Chefs

John Dicken

Several of the 'hot chefs' mention early culinary experiments on members of their families. 'Experiment' is a good word for John Dicken's first effort – though whether his sister's arteries were permanently hardened by the 12 scrambled eggs is not recorded. He himself loves a traditional English breakfast. He was head chef at Longueville Manor, Jersey, for five years, and has now reached the apogee of any chef's career – his own restaurant in Wethersfield, Essex, which has been open since October 1990.

Delice of Salmon with a Herb Crust

Serves 4

Herb crust
200 g (7 oz) fresh breadcrumbs
1 clove garlic, finely chopped
2 – 3 teaspoons finely chopped fresh parsley
2 – 3 teaspoons finely chopped fresh thyme
salt and pepper
about 4 tablespoons olive oil

Four 175 – 225 g (6 – 8 oz) fillet of salmon steaks
a little olive oil

Tomato sauce
50 ml (2 fl oz) olive oil
3 – 4 teaspoons lime juice
1 – 3 tablespoons water, according to taste
3 tomatoes, blanched, skinned, seeds removed and flesh chopped
10 cm (4 inch) piece cucumber, peeled, seeds removed and flesh cut into small dice
6 – 8 stoned black olives, chopped
2 – 3 teaspoons finely chopped fresh chives
1 teaspoon sugar (optional)

• To make the herb crust put the breadcrumbs, garlic, parsley, thyme and seasoning into a bowl. Add the olive oil. The mixture should be moist and not too dry or crumbly, so add a little more oil if necessary.

• Quickly seal the salmon steaks on both sides in a pan containing a little hot olive oil. When sealed, drain and place on a baking tray. Divide the herb crust between the four pieces of salmon and press gently on to the top surface. Cook in a pre-heated oven at 180°C (350°F), gas mark 4, and bake for about 15 – 20 minutes until fish is just tender.

• Meanwhile, to make the sauce, heat the oil in a pan. Carefully add the lime juice and a little water if you wish to reduce the acidity. Add the tomatoes, cucumber, olives, chives and sugar. Heat through gently for a few minutes.

• Remove the salmon from the oven and if the top needs extra browning, then place under a hot grill for a few seconds. Pour the tomato sauce on to the plates and place the salmon in the centre of each. Sprinkle with a few finely chopped chives if desired.

John Dicken, Dicken's Restaurant 9

Seafood and French Bean Tempura with Sauce Aioli

Serves 4 – 6

Marinade

1 tablespoon dry sherry
1 teaspoon nam pla (fish sauce) available in specialist, oriental or Thai stores
1 teaspoon soy sauce
1 teaspoon sesame oil
2 teaspoons sesame seeds
1 teaspoon Chinese five-spice powder
1/2 teaspoon chopped fresh root ginger
1/2 teaspoon chopped clove garlic
pinch sugar
salt and pepper
freshly ground Szechwan pepper

Fish

Assemble a selection of prepared fish according to choice, for example:
250 g (9 oz) skinned, filleted cod
250 g (9 oz) squid, cleaned
250 g (9 oz) filleted skate wing
250 g (9 oz) skinned filleted red mullet
250 g (9 oz) skinned filleted conger eel

Sauce aioli

125 g (4 oz) cooked potato, roughly chopped
2 egg yolks
2 cloves garlic, finely chopped
few threads saffron infused in 3 tablespoons warm water
200 ml (7 fl oz) olive oil
salt
cayenne pepper
a little water if required

Tempura

200 g (7 oz) plain flour or rice flour
100 g (3 1/2 oz) cornflour
30 g (1 oz) baking powder

oil for deep frying
250 g (9 oz) French beans, trimmed
salad leaves, such as oak leaf lettuce, frisée and lollo rosso
a little vinaigrette dressing
2 tomatoes, blanched, skinned, seeds removed and flesh chopped
freshly chopped parsley

• To make the marinade put all the ingredients into a bowl and mix together. Cut the fish into small, even-sized pieces. Mix with the marinade. Cover and keep in a cool place for no longer than two hours.

• To make the sauce aioli, put the potato, egg yolks and garlic into a food processor. Blend for a few seconds. Strain the saffron liquid and add to the egg yolk mixture. Blend briefly. With the processor switched on, slowly pour in the olive oil. Season with salt and cayenne pepper. Add a little water to adjust the consistency if desired.

• To make the tempura, sieve the flour, cornflour and baking powder into a bowl. Moisten the fish with a little water, then sprinkle lightly with the tempura flour making sure the pieces are coated. Heat the oil in a deep pan until a piece of day-old bread turns golden in a few seconds. Deep fry the fish in small batches for a few minutes until crisp and golden. Remove and drain on kitchen paper. Repeat this process with the French beans, moistening them first with a little water.

• Put a few salad leaves on to each plate. Trickle a little vinaigrette over the salad. Add a few chopped tomatoes to each one. Pour a ribbon of sauce aioli around the outside edge. Arrange the fish and French beans on top and serve sprinkled with chopped parsley.

Note – Szechwan peppercorns should be dry-roasted by cooking in a dry pan. Shake the pan and cook until they just start to smoke. Grind in a coffee grinder or small electric blender.

Roast Spring Rabbit with Rocket and Pine Kernels

Serves 4

4 legs of rabbit (or you can use boned chicken breasts, sliced almost
 through horizontally)
a little peanut or groundnut oil
150 g (5 oz) streaky bacon, cut in small strips and blanched in
 boiling water
75 g (2 ¹/₂ oz) pine kernels
1 clove garlic, finely chopped
4 small spring onions, finely chopped
125 g (4 oz) rocket salad (or use young spinach)
freshly grated nutmeg
salt and pepper
200 g (7 oz) crepinette (pigs' caul) washed or four pieces buttered
 foil
a little butter

Garnish
2 tablespoons oil
3 small turnips, peeled and cut into barrel shapes or dice
150 g (5 oz) streaky bacon, cut in small strips and blanched in
 boiling water
4 large prunes, soaked, stones removed and cut into strips
2 – 3 teaspoons finely chopped parsley
freshly grated nutmeg
salt and pepper

570 ml (1 pint) veal or chicken stock, reduced to 150 ml (¹/₄ pint) by
 boiling

• Carefully remove the bones from the rabbit legs. You could ask your butcher to do this for you. Carefully cut out any sinews and tendons.

• Heat 1 – 2 tablespoons peanut oil in a pan and add the bacon and cook until golden brown and crisp. Add the pine kernels and cook gently until they are lightly browned. Add the garlic, spring onion and rocket salad and cook until the rocket just starts to collapse. Season to taste with nutmeg, salt and pepper. Put the stuffing to one side and allow to become completely cold.

• Open out the boned rabbit legs and fill with the stuffing. Roll up and wrap with the crepinette. Brush with a little melted butter. Put into a baking tin and cook in a pre-heated oven at 190°C (375°F), gas mark 5, for 20 – 30 minutes.

• Meanwhile, to prepare the garnish, heat the oil in a pan and cook the turnips and bacon until golden brown. Add the prunes, parsley and seasoning and heat through gently. Heat the stock in a small pan.

• Remove the rabbit from the oven. Cut each one into slices and arrange on warm plates. Arrange the garnish to one side and pour over a little stock to moisten.

Cinnamon Parfait with Butterscotch Apples

Serves 6

4 egg yolks
85 g (3 oz) sugar
100 ml (3 1/2 fl oz) water
250 ml (9 fl oz) double cream, lightly whipped
1 teaspoon ground cinnamon, or to taste
150 ml (1/4 pint) double cream
125 g (4 oz) dark muscovado sugar
60 g (2 oz) butter
3 dessert apples, peeled, cored and cut into eighths
1 – 2 tablespoons calvados (optional)
crisp biscuits to serve

• To make the parfait, whisk the egg yolks in a bowl until thick. Put the sugar and water into a pan and heat gently to dissolve the sugar. Boil to 120°C (240°F) – soft ball stage. Remove from heat and whilst whisking the egg yolks pour the hot syrup slowly over the egg yolk mixture. Continue to whisk until the mixture is cold. Carefully fold in the whipped cream and cinnamon to taste. Pour into six individual ramekins and place in the freezer for at least six hours.

• Put the cream, sugar and butter into a saucepan and heat slowly. Add the apples and heat for a few minutes until the apple pieces are hot and just slightly tender.

• Remove the parfaits from the freezer. Dip each one briefly in hot water and unmould on to serving dishes, using a fork to help ease the parfait out of the dish.

• Remove the apples from the heat and add the calvados. Arrange a few apple slices on each dish next to the parfait and pour over a little sauce. Serve with crisp biscuits of your choice.

Fruit Salad Gratin with a Blackberry Sorbet

Serves 4 – 6

Blackberry sorbet
250 ml (9 fl oz) water
250 g (9 oz) caster sugar
500 g (18 fl oz) blackberry purée (made from about 900 g / 2 lb
   blackberries)

Custard cream
3 egg yolks
40 g (1 ¹/₂ oz) caster sugar
250 ml (9 fl oz) milk
¹/₂ vanilla pod, split
150 ml (5 fl oz) double cream

Biscuit tulips
2 large egg whites
125 g (4 oz) caster sugar
60 g (2 oz) plain sieved flour
100 g (3 ¹/₂ oz) unsalted butter, melted

Fruit salad
1 pear, peeled and lightly poached in water with sugar, cinnamon
   stick, bay leaf and a few peppercorns
1 orange, peel and pith removed and segmented
a few blackberries
a few raspberries
a few strawberries
1 kiwi fruit, peeled and cut into wedges

icing sugar

• To make the sorbet, put the sugar and water into a pan and heat gently until the sugar has dissolved. Bring to the boil and boil for one minute. Remove any scum. Allow to become cold. Mix the syrup and blackberry purée together and put into an electric sorbetière (ice-cream maker) and freeze.

• To make the custard cream, whisk the egg yolks and sugar together. Put the milk and vanilla pod into a pan and bring to the boil. Pour on to the eggs, stirring continuously. Pour the mixture back into the saucepan and cook over a low heat, stirring continuously, until the custard thickens and coats the back of the spoon. Strain the custard into a bowl. Lightly whip the double cream and fold gently into the cooled custard.

• To make the biscuit tulips, put the egg whites into a bowl and stir well together. Add the sugar and stir well. Add the flour and then slowly pour in the melted butter, beating well. If the mixture is too thick, add a little milk. Spoon a couple of tablespoons of mixture on to an oiled baking sheet or a baking tray lined with non-stick silicone paper. Spread out to a circle about 10 – 12.5 cm (4 – 5 inches) in diameter. Bake in a pre-heated oven at 150°C (300°F), gas mark 2, for 8 – 11 minutes. When cooked, remove, and using a palette knife quickly lift off the biscuit and place over a dariole mould. Cover with a slightly larger mould or cup to form the tulip. The biscuit quickly hardens as the mixture cools and can be removed from the mould. Continue in this way to make the other biscuit tulips. They can be made in advance and stored in an airtight tin.

• Arrange the prepared fruit attractively on each plate. Pour the custard cream over the fruit. Glaze under a hot grill. Meanwhile, fill each biscuit tulip with a scoop of blackberry sorbet. Place the tulip in the centre of the dish, sprinkle with icing sugar and serve at once.

Strawberry Cake

Serves 8

Sponge
3 eggs (size 2)
100 g (3 ¹/₂ oz) caster sugar
100 g (3 ¹/₂ oz) plain flour

Syrup
100 g (3 ¹/₂ oz) caster sugar
80 ml (3 fl oz) water
2 tablespoons kirsch

Filling
approx 225 g (8 oz) even-sized strawberries
3 egg yolks
60 g (2 oz) caster sugar
30 g (1 oz) plain flour, sieved
250 ml (9 fl oz) milk
1 teaspoon vanilla essence
2 tablespoons Kirsch
3 sheets (15 g / ¹/₂ oz) sheet gelatine, soaked in cold water for 15 minutes. Or use 15 g (¹/₂ oz) powder gelatine softened and dissolved in 3 – 4 tablespoons water
300 ml (11 fl oz) whipped double cream

Topping
2 tablespoons sieved apricot jam
250 g (9 oz) lime-coloured marzipan
icing roses and leaves or similar decorations of your choice

• To make the sponge, put the eggs and sugar into a bowl and whisk until thick and pale yellow in colour. The mixture should leave a trail when dropped from the whisk. Sieve the flour over the surface and gently fold in. Put the mixture into a buttered and lightly floured 20 cm (8 inch) cake ring or sandwich tin. Bake in a pre-heated oven at 190°C (375°F), gas mark 5, for about 20 minutes. Remove and allow to become cold.

• To make the syrup, put the sugar and water into a small pan. Heat gently until sugar has dissolved. Boil gently for one minute then remove from the heat. Stir in the kirsch.

• It is preferable to use a 20 cm (8 inch) x 5.5 cm (2 ¹/₄ inch) stainless steel cake ring, placed on a cake board, for this recipe. However, you can also use a loose-bottomed 20 cm (8 inch) cake tin and line the sides with non-stick silicone paper. Cut the sponge in half and place one half in the base of the ring or tin. Moisten with half the sugar syrup. Cut the strawberries in half and arrange around the outside of the cake ring with the cut side of the strawberries touching the ring. Put to one side.

• To make the filling, put the egg yolks and sugar into a bowl and whisk until pale. Add the flour and mix well. Boil the milk in a saucepan, and pour on to the egg mixture, stirring continuously. Pour the mixture through a sieve, back into the pan. Cook over a gentle heat, stirring continuously. Cook for two minutes. Remove from the heat. Stir in the kirsch and the drained, softened sheet gelatine and mix well. Pour into a bowl and allow to cool. When cool fold in the whipped cream and pour into the prepared cake ring.

• Place the remaining sponge on the top and moisten with the remaining syrup. Carefully spread the apricot jam over the sponge. Roll the marzipan out to a 20 cm (8 inch) round and place on top of the sponge.

• Chill for at least an hour to allow the filling to set. To remove the ring, place a warm damp cloth around the outside and then gently lift off.

• Decorate with icing roses and leaves or decorations of your choice.

Hot Chefs

Clive Fretwell

Clive Fretwell, chef at Le Manoir aux Quat' Saisons in Oxfordshire, started early – at the age of five he cooked dinner for his mother. Growing in experience, and bolstered also by a more favourable correlation between eye-level and work surface, he took his first job at the Hotel Jarl in Norway. He has been a chef at Le Manoir since 1984. His own taste-buds are particularly stimulated by oriental food.

Gateaux d'Aubergine (Aubergine Slices)

Serves 2

175 g (6 oz) – about ¹/₂ medium aubergine
100 ml (3 ¹/₂ fl oz) olive oil
1 medium courgette
salt and pepper
2 basil leaves, finely shredded
2 ripe tomatoes, preferably Italian plum
1 clove garlic, cut in half
125 g (4 oz) young spinach leaves

• Slice the aubergine into two equal rounds. Put into a hot frying pan with half the olive oil and colour on either side. Lower the heat, season and continue cooking until tender. Remove and drain on kitchen paper.

• Finely slice the courgettes and, together with the basil, fry in oil, without colouring, for about two minutes, until soft. Sprinkle with salt and pepper. Drain on kitchen paper.

• Put the tomatoes into boiling water for five seconds to blanch. Put at once into cold water. Remove skin. Cut in half and remove seeds. Place the prepared tomatoes in a small pan with a little olive oil and cook gently until the flesh begins to 'fall' but is not collapsed. Season with salt and pepper.

• In a saucepan heat a little oil with the garlic, add the spinach and cook, stirring. Allow most of the liquid from the spinach to evaporate. When the spinach has 'collapsed' drain on kitchen paper. Season. Remove the garlic pieces.

• You will need two 10 cm (4 inch) plastic rings to assemble this dish. Sections of new plastic drainpipe may be used, and they can be sterilised in boiling water if desired. Seal one end of the plastic rings with clingfilm.

• Build the gateaux in layers, starting with the spinach. Press it well over the base, leaving no gaps. Next arrange the courgettes slightly overlapping around the edge to form a 'well' into which you divide the cooked tomato. Finally, place the round of aubergine on to the top. Press down well. Trim the top of the aubergine flat with the mould if necessary. To serve, invert on to a plate and remove the ring and clingfilm, and serve at once.

Note – this dish can be prepared one day in advance and reheated in a microwave before serving.

Goat Cheese Soufflés

Serves 4

15 g (¹/₂ oz) butter
15 g (¹/₂ oz) plain flour
70 ml (2 ¹/₂ fl oz) milk
45 g (1 ¹/₂ oz) matured goat's cheese, or any cheese of your choice
pinch salt
pinch cayenne pepper
freshly ground black pepper
butter for greasing
60 g (2 oz) fine dried breadcrumbs
20 hazelnuts, toasted, skinned and ground
1 egg yolk
3 egg whites
lemon juice

Filling

40 g (1 ¹/₂ oz) matured goat's cheese, diced (or any cheese of your choice)

• Put the butter in a small pan and melt. Stir in the flour and cook for a minute. Gradually stir in the milk and bring to the boil. Cook gently and add the cheese. Stir until the cheese has melted. Remove from heat and add the seasonings.

• Butter four 10 x 5 cm (4 x 2 inch) ramekin dishes. Mix together the breadcrumbs and ground hazelnuts. Use to line the ramekin dishes.

• In a large bowl, whisk the egg whites to a soft peak. Whisk in a little lemon juice (about ¹/₆ of a lemon) and continue whisking until the egg whites are smooth and stiff. The lemon juice helps to prevent the egg white separating, and should be added half-way through whisking.

• Beat the egg yolk into the sauce mixture. Add a little whisked egg white to the sauce and beat well. To this add a third of the remaining egg whites. Carefully mix together, trying not to lose any volume of the egg. Now add this mixture to the remaining egg whites. Fold in very gently.

• Half fill the ramekins with soufflé mixture. Sprinkle the diced goat's cheese in the middle, then cover with the remaining mixture. Place the ramekins in a shallow roasting tin. Pour in 1 cm (¹/₂ inch) hot water. Cook in a pre-heated oven at 190°C (375 °F), gas mark 5, for ten minutes. Serve at once with a salad dressed with hazelnut or walnut dressing.

Note – If larger soufflé moulds are used, then the oven temperature should be reduced accordingly and the cooking time extended. Smaller soufflé moulds will be cooked at a higher temperature and have a shorter cooking time.

These soufflés may be made in advance and reheated. After baking, leave to cool for ten minutes. Then turn out carefully on to a lightly oiled baking sheet. To reheat, simply return to a hot oven or place under the grill for about five minutes to give a delicious crust.

Braised Fillet of Turbot with Cornish Scallops and Wild Asparagus

Serves 1

1 teaspoon butter
1 shallot, chopped
2 button mushrooms, sliced
2 tablespoons dry vermouth, or use any dry white wine
50 ml (2 fl oz) water
salt and pepper

one 175 g (6 oz) fillet of turbot, skinned
a little melted butter
lemon juice
2 large prepared Cornish scallops, with their corals
a little oil
125 g (4 oz) wild asparagus, or use fine asparagus, trimmed
1 tablespoon double cream
15 g (¹/₂ oz) butter, chilled and cut in small dice

- Heat the butter in a medium flameproof dish and cook the shallots for one to two minutes, without browning. Add the mushrooms and cook for a further minute. Add the vermouth and boil until reduced by half. Add the water and seasoning.

- Draw the pan off the heat and place the fish on top of the onions and mushrooms. Brush with a little melted butter and sprinkle over a little lemon juice. Cover lightly with a little buttered paper. Cook in a pre-heated oven at 180°C (350°F), gas mark 4, for six to eight minutes depending on the thickness of the fillets.

- Remove the corals from the scallops and poach in boiling water for 30 seconds. Remove. Trim and discard the grey part. Cut the coral into thin slices. Heat a little oil in a pan and quickly brown the corals for 30 seconds to a minute. Season, sprinkle with lemon juice and reserve.

- Cook the asparagus in boiling salted water for four to five minutes until just tender.

- Remove the fish from the oven. It should be slightly undercooked as it will finish cooking while resting. Strain off the stock from the fish and put into a pan. Cover the fish in its dish and keep warm. Heat the fish stock, stir in the cream. Add the butter and whisk well. Season with salt, pepper and lemon juice. Slice the white part of the scallops and add to the sauce. Simmer for one minute.

- Put the fish on a warmed plate. Pour the sauce over. Scatter the wild asparagus and corals attractively around the fish.

Fillet of Pan-fried John Dory
with Soused Aubergines Served with a Fresh Tomato Coulis

Serves 4

Soused aubergines
2 medium aubergines
about 200 ml (7 fl oz) olive oil
100 ml (3 ¹/₂ fl oz) water
50 ml (2 fl oz) white wine vinegar
1 tablespoon honey
salt and pepper
8 basil leaves, roughly chopped
2 sprigs thyme

Tomato coulis
100 ml (3 ¹/₂ fl oz) olive oil
2 pieces of zest of orange
1 piece of zest of lemon
2 sprigs thyme
6 basil leaves
5 – 6 ripe Italian plum tomatoes
salt and pepper

Four 225 g (8 oz) pieces skinned John Dory fillets (you could also use
    red mullet, sea bass, snapper, squid or cod)

4 tablespoons olive oil
knob of butter
squeeze lemon juice
salt and pepper

• Slice the aubergines into 3 mm (¹/₈ inch) slices. Heat some oil in a frying pan and fry them until lightly golden on both sides, adding more oil as necessary. Put in a shallow dish when cooked. Put the water, vinegar and honey into a saucepan and bring to the boil. Pour over the fried aubergine slices. Add seasoning, basil and thyme and toss gently together. Allow to infuse for a couple of hours.

• To prepare the tomato coulis, put the olive oil, orange and lemon zests, thyme and basil into a saucepan. Gently warm through. On no account should the oil boil at any time. Infuse for five minutes. Strain through a sieve. Put this scented oil to one side. Put the tomatoes into a food processor or blender and process until liquid. Put the tomatoes into a saucepan through a fine sieve.

• Place the fish fillets into a pan containing the oil heated with a little butter. Lightly brown on both sides. Reduce the heat and let the fish finish cooking through gently. The flesh should be firm but moist. Season with lemon juice and salt and pepper.

• Gently reheat the aubergines and marinade in a frying pan. Gently heat the sieved tomatoes in a pan and slowly whisk in the scented oil.

• Arrange a few aubergine slices on each plate. Place a piece of fish on top. Surround with the tomato coulis and finish with a little olive oil dribbled into the coulis for taste and decoration.

Turbot and Salmon Fillets Wrapped in Savoy Cabbage Leaves

Serves 1

2 large leaves savoy or green cabbage
salt and pepper
2 pieces fillet of turbot, each 6 cm (2 1/4 inch) square and 1 cm
    (1/2 inch) thick
1 piece fillet of wild salmon, 6 cm (2 1/4 inch) square x 1 cm (1/2 inch)
    thick
a little melted butter
squeeze lemon juice
4 small sprigs dill
1 small shallot, finely chopped
1 tablespoon white wine vinegar
3 tablespoons dry white wine
2 teaspoons water
1 tablespoon cream
100 g (3 1/2 oz) unsalted butter, chilled and diced
lemon juice
salt and pepper

Garnish
1 tablespoon caviar
sprig dill
a little 'turned' or diced cucumber

• Put the cabbage leaves into a large pan of boiling, salted water and cook for three to four minutes until they become pliable. Drain and refresh in cold water. Remove and pat dry. Remove the centre vein from each leaf.

• Season the fish fillets. Brush them with a little melted butter which has had a squeeze of lemon juice added to it. Sandwich the salmon between the turbot, adding sprigs of dill to each layer.

• Brush the cabbage leaves with lemon butter and season well. Place the parcel of turbot and salmon in the centre of one leaf. Wrap the cabbage leaf around the fish. Invert it and place it on to the second cabbage leaf. Wrap this leaf around the first. Wrap tightly in clingfilm and refrigerate. The parcel may be kept overnight at this stage, if required.

Cook in a steamer for 10 – 12 minutes and then leave to rest for three to four minutes before serving.

• Meanwhile, to make the sauce, put the shallot, wine vinegar and white wine into a pan. Boil and reduce to about 1 teaspoon of liquid. Add the water and cream and stir well. Over a gentle heat, whisk in the butter, a little at a time, to form a smooth emulsion. Season with lemon juice and salt and pepper.

• To serve, remove the clingfilm from the cooked parcel and, using a sharp knife, cut across the middle without cutting through the bottom layer of cabbage and part the edges to reveal the colours inside.

Place the opened parcel on the plate and pour the sauce around the edge. Garnish with caviar, fresh dill and cucumber.

Norfolk Squabs Baked in a Salt Pastry Crust

Serves 4

Four 350 g (12 oz) corn-fed pigeons
1 tablespoon butter
1 tablespoon groundnut oil

Salt paste

1 kg (2 $^1/_4$ lbs) strong white flour, plus extra for dusting
600 g (1 lb 5 oz) fine table salt
7 egg whites
approx 300 ml ($^1/_2$ pint) water to bind
egg wash (2 egg yolks beaten with 1 tablespoon milk and a large
    pinch caster sugar)
a handful of rock salt and 8 cloves for decoration

Sauce

neck and wings of squabs
a little oil
2 teaspoons unsalted butter
2 shallots, finely chopped
60 g (2 oz) button mushrooms
3 tablespoons ruby port
4 tablespoons dry Madeira
200 ml (7 fl oz) homemade dark chicken stock
salt and pepper
2 tablespoons whipping cream
truffle juice and 15 g ($^1/_2$ oz) truffle (optional)
1 teaspoon arrowroot mixed with a little water

• Prepare the pigeons as for roasting. You can ask the butcher to do this and he should cut off the feet, wings and neck and remove the wishbone. Reserve the last three items for the sauce. Truss the birds. Heat the butter and oil in a pan and sear well on each leg side (but not the breasts) for three to four minutes each. Leave to cool.

• To make the paste, put the flour, salt and egg white into a mixer. (Or you can do it by hand but it takes longer.) Mix at slow speed for one to two minutes. Slowly add the water until it forms a smooth paste. Mix for five to ten minutes to form a smooth dough.

• On a floured work surface, divide the pastry into four. Roll out one piece to a thickness of 7 mm ($^1/_4$ inch). Place a pigeon on top and cut a square with a 5 cm (2 inch) border around the bird. Moisten the edges and lay the pigeon, breast side down, on to the paste. Wrap up the pigeon completely, ensuring there are no holes. From the trimmings cut two teardrop shapes about 12 cm (5 inches) long for the wings and mould a head for the body. Moisten the wings and head with a little water and secure on to the body. Brush all over with egg wash and use two cloves for eyes. Press a little rock salt into the salt crust breast of the pigeon. Repeat for the three other birds. Place on a lightly oiled baking tray and bake in a pre-heated oven at 230°C (450°F), gas mark 8, for 25 minutes. Allow to rest for five minutes before carving.

• To make the sauce, chop up the winglets, wishbones and neck trimmings. Sear in a hot pan with a little oil, stirring occasionally. In another saucepan, heat the butter and cook the shallots for two to three minutes without browning. Add the mushrooms and cook for a minute. Add the port and Madeira and reduce by half. Drain the chopped pigeon bones and add to the sauce together with the chicken stock. Bring to the boil and simmer for 10 – 15 minutes. Season. Stir in the cream and truffle and juice if used. Heat gently for a minute. Sieve into a clean pan. Add the blended arrowroot and bring to the boil, stirring.

• To serve, break open the salt crust and discard and remove the pigeons. Remove trussing and cut each one into pieces. Serve with the sauce.

This dish may be garnished with small slices of foie gras cooked until golden and spiked with sherry vinegar; rosti potatoes; and lightly sautéed wild mushrooms.

Roast Breast of Barbary Duckling with Jasmine Sauce

Serves 6

3 ducklings, 1.5 kg (3 ½ lb) each
200 ml (7 fl oz) Pineau des Charentes or cherry brandy
400 ml (14 fl oz) red wine, such as cabernet sauvignon
600 ml (1 pint) fresh orange juice
30 g (1 oz) sugar
15 g (½ oz) unsalted butter
juice 1 lime
1.2 litre (2 pints) cold water
4 tablespoons meat glaze or rich stock (optional)
30 g (1 oz) jasmine tea leaves
1 teaspoon arrowroot, blended with a little water
salt and pepper
60 g (2 oz) golden sultanas, soaked in hot jasmine tea for four hours

• Remove the neck, wishbone and winglets from the duck. Then remove the legs and the backbone, leaving the breasts on the bone. Chop the winglets, neck and backbone into small pieces. Put in a roasting pan (without any fat or oil) and roast in a hot oven at 230°C (450°F), gas mark 8, for 10 – 20 minutes, stirring occasionally until golden brown. Remove. Strain through a sieve to remove all the fat. Place the browned bones in a saucepan.

• Pour the Pineau des Charentes and red wine together into a separate pan and boil until reduced to 200 ml (7 fl oz). Put the orange juice into another pan and boil until reduced to 200 ml (7 fl oz). Cook the butter and sugar in a pan until they caramelise. Remove from the heat and stir in the lime juice. (Take care at this point as the caramel will bubble up and spit.)

• Add the cold water to the duck bones. Bring to the boil and cook for about 20 minutes until reduced to about 300 ml (½ pint). Add the reduced wine, reduced orange juice, lime flavoured caramel and meat stock if used. Reduce by about half. Add the jasmine tea. Simmer for a few minutes. Sieve into a clean pan. Thicken with a little blended arrowroot.

• Meanwhile, score the duck breasts lightly with a sharp knife and then place, skin side down, into a hot frying pan. No fat is needed as there is plenty in the duck. Cook until the skins are crisp and golden brown. Put the breasts, skin side up, into a roasting pan and cook in the oven at 220°C (425°F), gas mark 7, for 10 – 15 minutes. Allow to rest for five minutes to 'relax' the meat.

• Gently warm the sultanas in the jasmine tea and reheat the sauce. Remove duck breasts from the bone. Season and slice the meat. Place on the warm plates. Drain the sultanas and scatter around the meat. Pour over the sauce. Garnish with filo pastry parcels filled with candied shallots and lightly steamed cabbage leaves topped with pan-fried slices of foie gras.

Filo Parcels

15 g (½ oz) unsalted butter
18 small shallots, peeled and roughly chopped
salt and pepper
2 teaspoons fresh chopped coriander
six 12 cm (5 inch) squares filo pastry
6 strips leek or spring onions, blanched
butter

• Melt the butter in a pan. Add the shallots and cook, uncovered, over a moderate heat for about ten minutes. Cover with a lid and continue cooking for a further 10 – 20 minutes, stirring occasionally until golden brown. Season. Add the coriander and cool.

• Arrange the filo pastry squares (two or three layers to each square) on a baking sheet. Place a little onion mixture in the centre of each. Wrap into small parcels and tie with leek 'ribbons'. Brush with a little melted butter and cook in the oven at 220°C (425°F), gas mark 7, for five to ten minutes until crisp and golden.

La Truffière de Chocolat (Chocolate Mousse)

Serves 5–6

Biscuit base
2 egg whites
60 g (2 oz) caster sugar
2 egg yolks
60 g (2 oz) plain flour, sieved

Syrup
2 tablespoons water
15 g (^{1}/$_2$ oz) caster sugar
1 tablespoon rum

Mousse
125 g (4 oz) extra bitter chocolate
200 ml (7 fl oz) whipping cream

To finish
1 tablespoon unsweetened cocoa powder

• To make the biscuit base, beat the egg whites until they reach soft peaks. Add the sugar gradually, continuously beating. When all the sugar is added, fold in the egg yolks. Fold in the flour carefully. Line a baking tray with non-stick silicone paper. Pour the mixture over and spread out to 1 cm (just under ^{1}/$_2$ inch) thick. Bake in a pre-heated oven at 230°C (450°F), gas mark 8, for six to eight minutes. Allow to cool.

• To make the syrup, put the water in a small saucepan and add the sugar. Bring to the boil, skim off any impurities then simmer for about one minute until reduced by half. Cool, then add rum.

• Use either a pastry ring 15 cm x 3.5 cm (6 inch by 1 ^{1}/$_2$ inch) and a cardboard base the same diameter, or a loose-based 15 cm (6 inch) cake tin. Use the ring or cake tin base to cut a circle from the biscuit base. With a pastry brush, dampen the biscuit base with the syrup. Place the biscuit base on to the cardboard base on a tray, and fit the pastry ring over it (or put the biscuit base in the bottom of the cake tin). Put to one side.

• To make the chocolate mousse, break the chocolate into pieces and melt in a bowl placed over a pan of hot (not boiling) water. Stir and make sure that all of the chocolate has melted, reaching a temperature of 40°C (104°F) or 'hand hot'.

• In a large bowl, whip the cream until thick but still loose in texture. Briskly mix one third of the whipped cream into the hot chocolate, then pour the mixture into the bulk of the whipped cream. Fold in gently with a spatula.

• Pour the mixture into the ring on top of the biscuit. Smooth the top and refrigerate for at least two hours. Sprinkle the surface of the mousse with sieved cocoa powder.

• Place a warm damp cloth around the ring for a few seconds, lift the ring off and serve.

Paquet Surprise de Manoir (Parcel of Lemon Parfait)

Serves 4

Candied lemon zests
zest from 1 $^1/_2$ lemons
juice from 2 lemons
30 g (1 oz) sugar

Lemon parfait
3 egg whites
60g (2 oz) powder glucose (from a chemist)
60 g (2 oz) caster sugar
1 tablespoon cold water
50 ml (2 fl oz) lemon juice
100 ml (4 fl oz) double cream, whipped

Biscuits
60 g (2 oz) soft, unsalted butter
75 g (2 $^1/_2$ oz) icing sugar
60 g (2 oz) egg whites, at room temperature
pinch salt
60 g (2 oz) plain flour
a little melted plain chocolate (optional)

Cherry coulis
150 g (5 oz) whole cherries
60 g (2 oz) sugar
100 ml (4 fl oz) water
150 g (5 oz) stoned cherries
1 clove
few pieces cinnamon stick
2 tablespoons sugar
dash of kirsch

• To make the candied lemon zest, chop the zest into fine julienne strips. Cover with cold water, bring to the boil, then rinse under cold running water. Repeat this process. The third time, add the juice of one lemon, the sugar and sufficient cold water barely to cover the zests. Bring to the boil, remove any scum and then simmer for five minutes. Remove from the heat and stir in the remaining lemon juice.

• To make the lemon parfait, whisk the egg whites. Put the glucose, sugar and water into a small pan and bring to the boil. Boil to 120°C (240°F) – soft ball. Gradually pour the syrup on to the egg whites whilst still whisking. Gradually add the lemon juice, whilst still whisking and continue whisking until cool. Mix a third of the egg-white mixture with the whipped double cream and candied lemon zests. Return to the remaining two-thirds of the egg-white mixture and carefully fold together. Line a shallow container with non-stick paper. Fill with the lemon parfait and freeze overnight.

• Make a template from the lid of a plastic container in the form of a cross 15 cm (6 inches) in length each way and 6 cm (2 $^1/_2$ inches) in width.

15 cm
6 cm

• To make the biscuit, mix together the butter and icing sugar. Add the egg whites and the salt and flour and mix until smooth. Place the cross template on to a tray lined with non-stick silicone paper and spread the biscuit paste over it. Using melted chocolate pipe 'parcel strings' on to the biscuit and remove template. In a pre-heated oven at 180°C (350°F), gas mark 4, bake the biscuit for five to six minutes. Cool the biscuit for a minute then remove to another baking sheet. Repeat this process three more times to make four crosses.

• To make the cherry coulis, put the whole cherries (do not remove stones) sugar and water into a pan, bring to the boil and simmer for four minutes. Liquidise and then sieve. Put the stoned cherries, clove and cinnamon, sugar and coulis into a pan. Bring to the boil, add the kirsch and simmer for two minutes. Remove from heat and allow to cool.

• To serve, reheat each biscuit in the oven. Cut a piece of lemon parfait into a 6 cm (2 $^1/_2$ inch) square, place into the centre of the warmed biscuit and quickly fold over the edges to make a parcel. Hold in place for two seconds until the biscuit cools. Spoon a little of the fresh cherries and coulis on to the centre of the plate and place the parcel on top.

Tarte aux Poires (Pear Tart) with Vanilla Custard

Serves 4

Pastry
60 g (2 oz) unsalted butter, softened
40 g (1 ½ oz) icing sugar
1 egg yolk
small pinch salt
125 g (4 oz) plain flour, sieved
1 – 3 teaspoons water
butter for greasing

Almond cream
60 g (2 oz) unsalted butter, softened
60 g (2 oz) icing sugar
60 g (2 oz) ground almonds
1 egg
1 tablespoon whipping cream
1 tablespoon rum (optional)

4 pear halves, peeled, poached and cored

icing sugar

• To make the pastry, put the butter into a bowl and cream with a spoon. Add the icing sugar, egg yolk and salt and mix well. Add the flour and gradually beat into the mixture adding enough water to mix to a smooth paste. Lightly flour a work surface and place the dough on it. Knead with the palms of your hands until well blended. Wrap in clingfilm and chill in the refrigerator for at least six hours.

• Grease a 20 cm (8 inch) fluted flan tin with a removable base. Roll the dough out on a lightly floured surface and line the flan tin. Make a parcel using some spare dough wrapped in a piece of clingfilm to press the dough well into the corners of the flan tin. Trim the edge and chill for an hour.

• To make the almond cream, put the butter, icing sugar, ground almonds and egg into a bowl and mix well together. Stir in the cream and rum, if used. Spread the almond cream on to the bottom of the tart. Cut each pear into slices horizontally. Place the four pear halves to form a cross on top of the almond cream. Place the tart in a pre-heated oven at 180°C (350°F), gas mark 4, for 40 minutes.

• Remove and allow to cool. Serve sprinkled with icing sugar and accompany with vanilla custard.

Vanilla Custard

Makes 500 ml (18 fl oz)

6 egg yolks
75 g (2 ½ oz) caster sugar
1 large vanilla pod, split lengthways, scraped and seeds
   spread back on pod
500 ml (18 fl oz) milk

• In a large mixing bowl, cream together the egg yolks and sugar until a pale straw colour.

• Combine the vanilla pod and milk in a heavy based saucepan, bring to the boil and simmer for about five minutes. Draw off the heat and cool for 30 seconds.

• Pour the milk on to the eggs and sugar, whisking continuously, then return the mixture to the saucepan over a medium heat and stir to bind the custard until it coats the back of a wooden spoon.

• Strain immediately into a china bowl and stir for a few minutes as the custard cools down. Place in the refrigerator until required.

Hot Chefs

Mark Gregory

As a lesson in making a virtue of necessity, the career of Mark Gregory, whose mother's efforts in the kitchen reportedly left something (edibility?) to be desired, is hard to beat. He is now head chef at the exclusive hotel and restaurant, Brocket Hall, in Hertfordshire, which is also the home of Lord Brocket and has been in the Brocket family since 1290. Mark Gergory's taste in food is rather less exclusive, though doubtless no less discriminating: he can't stand oysters, and his favourite meal was bought in San Francisco for $3.50: duck with noodles.

Lobster Coromandel

Serves 4

Four 250 g (8 – 9 oz) lobster tails (preferably raw)
a little butter
paprika pepper
salt
nutmeg
cayenne pepper
1 egg white
about 300 ml (11 fl oz) double cream
85 g (3 oz) sliced smoked salmon, cut in strips
2 teaspoons truffle trimmings, optional
8 spears fine asparagus, blanched
small bunch chives

Sauce

100 ml (3 ¹/₂ fl oz) dry white wine
1 shallot, finely chopped
2 teaspoons lemon juice
200 ml (7 fl oz) fish stock
200 ml (7 fl oz) whipping cream
pinch nutmeg
1 ripe avocado, sieved
salt and pepper

Vegetable garnish

1 large potato, peeled and cut into 4 'turned' potatoes
1 large carrot, peeled and cut into 8 'turned' carrots
2 courgettes, cut into 8 'turned' courgettes
a few 'turned' mushrooms
a little lemon juice
4 teaspoons chopped tomato flesh
few sprigs mint

• Using a pair of kitchen scissors, cut away the transparent underside of the lobster tails. Remove the flesh carefully in one piece. Remove the dark-coloured vein that runs through the lobster and discard. Cut the tails in half horizontally. Put the tops (pink side) in the freezer for a little while to chill and reserve the bottoms (white side) for later.

• Clean the lobster tail shells and rub the inside with butter. Sprinkle well on the inside with paprika pepper.

• Remove the lobster tail tops from the freezer and chop roughly. Put it into a food processor and add a little salt, nutmeg and cayenne. Process until the mixture becomes a stiff paste. Blend in the egg white, a little at a time. Add the cream and process until smooth. Remove and pass through a fine sieve into a cold bowl.

• Using a palette knife, spread a little of the lobster mousseline over the inside of the prepared lobster shells. Lay the strips of salmon, truffle, asparagus and chives evenly along the tails. Cover with more mousseline and finally place the remaining bottom halves of lobster in each tail so as to regain their original shape. Wrap each tail in buttered foil, place in a steamer and cook for 15 – 18 minutes.

• To make the sauce, put the wine, shallots and lemon juice into a pan. Reduce by two-thirds. Add the fish stock and reduce again by three-quarters. Add the cream and bring to the boil, stirring. Add the nutmeg and avocado and whisk in thoroughly. Season to taste. Do not let the sauce boil once the avocado purée has been added.

• Cook the 'turned' vegetables in boiling salted water with a little lemon juice until just tender. Drain.

• Remove the lobster tails from the steamer. Allow to rest for five minutes before gently removing from their shells. Carve each into four for serving.

• Pour a little sauce on to each plate. Arrange the lobster on top. Arrange the vegetable garnish attractively to one side and serve at once.

Mark Gregory, Brocket Hall 27

Sushi and Soba Salad

Serves 6 – 8

Sushi rice

300 g (11 oz) short-grain rice
7.5 cm (3 inch) piece konbu seaweed
350 ml (12 fl oz) water
1 tablespoon sake or dry white wine
2 1/2 tablespoons rice vinegar or white wine vinegar
1 tablespoon caster sugar
1/2 teaspoon salt

Sushi

5 – 6 sheets nori
450 g (1 lb) cooked sushi rice
Wasabi paste (Japanese horseradish) (optional)
350 g (12 oz) smoked salmon or cooked king prawns, smoked
     chicken, etc
long thin strips peeled cucumber and de-seeded peppers, marinated
     for two hours in equal quantities of rice vinegar, sugar and water
     with a pinch of salt
egg pancake, cut into strips (optional)
Daikon (mooli) cut into strips
Japanese naturally brewed soy sauce

• To make the sushi rice, wash the rice under cold water. Place in a pan with the konbu, water and sake. Cover with a tight lid and bring to the boil. Remove the konbu and reserve, replace the lid and cook over a low heat for 15 minutes. Then switch off the heat, leaving the lid on, and allow the rice to steam for a further 10 – 15 minutes.

• Put the hot rice into a bowl. Gently and quickly mix in the vinegar, sugar and salt. Spread out on a tray and cover with clingfilm, which has been pierced a few times, or a damp tea towel. Cool completely.

• To assemble the sushi you will need a thin wooden mat, or a tea towel or sheet of clingfilm. Lay the nori out on the mat. Leaving 5 cm (2 inches) of nori clear at one end, spoon a thin line of sushi rice across the width of the nori. Spread with a very little wasabi paste if desired. Cut the salmon (or whatever you are using) into long thin strips and lay a few along the rice. Do the same with the strips of cucumber, peppers, egg pancake and daikon. Spoon a little more rice on top. Sprinkle the nori with a little water. Fold over the 5 cm (2 inch) band of nori and roll up tightly as for a Swiss roll, using the mat to keep it tight.

• Once rolled up, leave the sushi wrapped up for about ten minutes. Then unroll and with a sharp knife, cut into 2.5 cm (1 inch) pieces and serve with soy sauce and a little wasabi paste.

/cont.

Soba Salad

Serves 4 – 6

200 g (7 oz) soba (buckwheat) noodles

Dressing
200 ml (7 fl oz) dashi (purchased ready made in a bottle)
2 teaspoons sugar
2 tablespoons Japanese naturally brewed soy sauce
2 tablespoons rice vinegar
2 tablespoons mirin (rice wine for cooking, you can use dry sherry)
1 tablespoon sake (or dry white wine)
1 tablespoon sesame oil
150 ml (1/4 pint) sunflower oil

2 handfuls young spinach leaves, washed and dried

30 – 60 g (1 – 2 oz) wakame seaweed, soaked in cold water for five minutes then blanched for 30 seconds in boiling water, then chopped
1 bunch watercress
30 g (1 oz) finely sliced spring onions
60 g (2 oz) bean sprouts
30 g (1 oz) hijiki seaweed, soaked

• Bring a large pan of salted water to the boil. Put the soba noodles into the pan making sure they do not stick together. Cook for four to five minutes until 'al dente'. Drain and immediately plunge the noodles into ice-cold water. When cold, drain well.

• Put the dashi, sugar, soy sauce, rice vinegar, mirin, sake, sesame and sunflower oils into a bowl and mix well together.

• Place the cooked soba noodles in the base of a large serving bowl. Arrange the spinach, wakame, watercress, spring onion, bean sprouts and hijiki on top. Pour plenty of dressing over the salad and serve at once.

Arabic Chicken

Serves 6

Stuffing

175 g (6 oz) couscous
1 small chilli, de-seeded and finely chopped
2 teaspoons ground cumin
2 teaspoons sammak (a red coloured spice that can be bought in shops that specialise in Middle Eastern and Jewish food) (optional)
40 g (1 1/2 oz) raisins
1 tablespoon lemon zest strips, blanched
2 tablespoons chopped flat parsley
1 tablespoon chopped mint
3 tablespoons olive oil
175 ml (6 fl oz) warm water
salt and pepper

1.2 kg (2 3/4 lb) chicken, boned (your butcher will do this)
about 150 g (5 oz) hummus
a little olive oil
150 ml (1/4 pint) sour cream
1 – 2 teaspoons honey
1/2 teaspoon ground cinnamon

Garnish

onions, sliced and deep fried until dark golden brown
fresh parsley

● To make the stuffing, put the couscous, chilli, cumin, sammak, raisins, lemon, parsley and mint into a bowl. Mix together the oil and water and pour over the couscous. Season and leave to soak for about ten minutes.

● Open out the prepared chicken, and make a few slashes in the flesh to prevent it from 'tightening' too much during cooking. Season with salt and pepper. Spread the hummus over the chicken. Lay the couscous stuffing along the centre and fold over each side of the chicken to enclose the stuffing completely. It should be in a long thin roll. Use a large loaf tin, or similar shaped dish, to contain the shape of the roll. Line with buttered paper. (If you do not have a suitable container, then tie the roll up with string at 5 cm (2 inch) intervals and cook in a roasting tin.)

● Brush the chicken with oil and place in a pre-heated oven at 220°C (425°F), gas mark 7, for ten minutes, then reduce heat to 190°C (375°F), gas mark 5, and cook for a further hour or until golden and cooked through. Leave to rest for a few minutes before removing from the tin.

● To make the sauce mix together the sour cream, honey and cinnamon. Serve the chicken in slices, accompanied with the sauce and deep fried onions. Garnish with parsley.

Hummus

350 g (12 oz) chickpeas, soaked overnight
1 teaspoon bicarbonate of soda
2 – 3 cloves garlic, chopped
1 teaspoon salt
1/2 teaspoon ground cumin
100 g (3 1/2 oz) tahini (sesame seed paste)
juice 2 lemons

● Cook the chickpeas in boiling salted water, with the bicarbonate of soda, for about one hour or until tender. Drain and reserve a little of the cooking liquid.

● Put the chickpeas into a food processor with the garlic, salt, cumin, tahini and lemon juice. Process to produce a soft paste. Add a little cooking liquid if the mixture is too dry and mix to a smooth cream.

Sweet or Savoury Tempura

Both serve 4 – 6

Tempura Batter

3 egg yolks
400 ml (14 fl oz) iced water
250 g (9 oz) plain flour

• Put the egg yolks into a bowl and gently whisk in the water.

• Add the flour and whisk again. Do not over-whisk: if anything the batter should be a little lumpy.

Fresh fruits tempura

1 quantity of tempura batter
2 tablespoons finely chopped glacé stem ginger
plain flour for dusting
a selection of prepared fruits such as apples, bananas, pears, peaches, apricots, pineapple, etc
oil for deep frying
maple syrup

• Stir the chopped ginger into the batter.

• Cut the fruit into thin, even-sized pieces. Dust the fruit pieces in flour and shake off any excess.

• Heat the oil in a deep pan until a piece of day-old bread turns golden in a few seconds.

• Dip the fruits into the batter and deep fry in small batches until crisp and golden. Serve with maple syrup for dipping.

Savoury tempura

1 quantity of tempura batter
plain flour for dusting
a selection of prepared vegetables such as peppers, carrots, mushrooms, daikon (mooli) courgettes, mangetout, etc, cut into thin slices or strips – you will need about 450 g (1 lb) in total
boneless chicken, or veal, salmon, white fish etc, cut into small even-sized strips. You will need about 450 g (1 lb) in total.
oil for deep frying

Dipping sauce
200 ml (7 fl oz) Japanese naturally brewed soy sauce
125 g (4 oz) dried bonito flakes
1 tablespoon sugar
1 tablespoon sake or dry white wine

Garnish
a few udon (Japanese wheat) noodles
small piece nori (seaweed), dampened.

• Put the batter in a large bowl. Dust the pieces of vegetables and meat or fish with flour and shake off the excess.

• Heat the oil in a deep pan until a piece of day-old bread turns golden in a few seconds. Dip the vegetable and meat pieces in the batter and deep fry in small batches for a few minutes until crisp and golden. Serve garnished with a udon fan and accompanied with a dipping sauce.

• To make the sauce, put all the ingredients into a small pan. Slowly bring to the boil and simmer for about ten minutes. Strain and allow to cool.

• To make the udon fan, take a few noodles, bind them at one end with a piece of dampened nori. Dip in the tempura batter and deep fry until golden.

Picasso Ice-Cream

The first thing to point out with this recipe is that there are no set ingredients. Simply decide what you like, or perhaps just use what there is in the fridge, and be creative! Here is a suggestion to start you off.

chocolate sauce
strawberry purée
blackberry purée
kiwi fruit purée
strawberry ice-cream (see recipe below)
passion fruit curd (see recipe below)
pieces of sablée or shortbread biscuits cut in an abstract fashion
crushed meringue pieces
fresh strawberries, raspberries, etc
whipped double cream
icing sugar (optional)

Strawberry ice-cream

275 g (10 oz) caster sugar
50 ml (2 ¹/₂ fl oz) water
4 large egg whites
425 ml (15 fl oz) double cream, lightly whipped
700 g (1 ¹/₂ lb) strawberries, puréed in a food processor or blender

• Put the sugar and water in a pan and heat gently until the sugar has dissolved. Bring to the boil and cook to 120°C (240°F) soft ball stage.

• One minute or so before the sugar is cooked, whisk the egg whites until stiff. Then, slowly pour the hot syrup on to the egg whites, whisking continuously. Continue whisking until the meringue becomes cool.

• Put the lightly whipped double cream into a large bowl and fold in the strawberry purée. Then fold in the cooled meringue mixture, taking care to keep the mixture light. Pour into a suitable container and freeze until required.

• Pour, spoon or pipe the chocolate sauce and fruit purées on to each plate so that all the colours blend and look pleasing.

• Place three balls or scoops of ice-cream on each plate and top with a little passion fruit curd. Arrange the biscuits and/or meringues over the ice-cream.

• Decorate the plate with whole strawberries etc and a spoonful of whipped cream. Sprinkle with icing sugar and serve at once.

Passion fruit curd

Makes 1 jar

1 unwaxed lemon
5 passion fruits
125 g (4 oz) unsalted butter, cut into cubes
275 g (10 oz) caster sugar
5 medium eggs, well beaten

• Remove half of the rind from the lemon with a zester (or grate finely) and squeeze only one half for the juice. Chop the lemon zest finely.

• Cut the passion fruits in half. Scoop out the flesh and juice and push through a sieve, collecting the juice. Reserve a few of the seeds.

• Put the passion fruit juice, lemon zest and juice into a bowl over a pan of simmering water. Add the caster sugar and butter and stir until melted.

• Pour in the beaten eggs whilst stirring continuously. Do not let the mixture boil, or it will curdle. Stir and cook the mixture until it thickens. Stir in some of the reserved seeds.

• Pour into a clean, dry, warm jar. Cover. It will keep in the fridge for about two months.

Hot Chefs

Alastair Little

Alastair Little: man and Soho restaurant. The former, chef and co-proprietor of the latter, is one of those fortunate enough to have made a successful career out of his hobby. His first job was as a waiter in a wine bar where Dudley Moore was providing the music. Dud is a man arguably even more fortunate, having made a hobby out of his career – an option, his clients fervently hope, that is not tempting his erstwhile colleague. What Alastair Little *is* irresistibly tempted by, apparently, is casseroled eel with crispy pork and garlic.

Tortillas and Vegetable Mexican Garnishes

Tortillas
1.1 litre (2 pints) plain strong flour
60 g (2 oz) lard
30 g (1 oz) fresh yeast, mixed with 3 tablespoons tepid water
1 teaspoon salt
approx 300 ml (1/2 pint) tepid water

Guacamole
1 very ripe avocado
salt and pepper
juice 1 lemon or lime

Salsa
2 red onions, roughly chopped
2 cloves garlic
1 large red chilli
225 g (8 oz) cherry tomatoes
few sprigs fresh coriander
1 – 2 tablespoons lemon juice
approx 150 ml (1/4 pint) tomato juice

sour cream
finely chopped fresh spinach

• To make the dough, put the flour (measured in a measuring jug) and the lard into a food processor. Add the yeast and salt and pulse briefly to mix everything together. Add about 300 ml (1/2 pint) water and process until the dough forms a single ball. Add more water if necessary. Turn out into a bowl, cover with a cloth and leave to rise for about an hour, or until double in size.

• To prepare the garnishes, first make the guacamole by mashing together, with a fork, the avocado, seasoning and lemon juice. Put into a small bowl.

• To make the salsa, put the onions, garlic, chilli, tomatoes, coriander and lemon juice into a food processor and pulse briefly to give a coarse textured sauce. Add the tomato juice and season with lots of salt. Put into a bowl.

• Put the sour cream into one small bowl and the chopped spinach into another.

• Roll the risen dough either through a pasta machine or with a rolling pin, until very thin. Cut into large rounds. Heat a heavy based frying pan or griddle or use a solid top grill. Cook the tortillas for about 30 seconds on each side until they are puffed up and golden. Serve immediately stuffed with the vegetable garnishes.

Chicken Wrapped in Parma Ham and Savoy Cabbage

Serves 4

Stock

1.1 litre (2 pints) boiling water
2 chicken stock cubes
1 stick celery, finely sliced
2 carrots, peeled and finely sliced
1 leek, finely sliced
small piece celeriac, chopped
1 bay leaf
2 – 3 black peppercorns

8 savoy cabbage leaves
8 slices Parma ham
4 chicken breast fillets
200 g (7 oz) butter
freshly ground black pepper

• Bring the water to the boil in a pan and add the stock cubes. Add the chopped vegetables, bay leaf and peppercorns. Simmer gently for one hour. Strain through a sieve.

• Cut the tough centre stalk out of the cabbage leaves. Blanch the leaves in boiling salted water for about 30 seconds. Refresh in cold water and drain.

• Butter four pieces of aluminium foil. Place two cabbage leaves on each piece of foil. Top with two slices of Parma ham. Put a chicken breast on top of the ham. Top each piece of chicken with 30 g (1 oz) butter. Season with pepper. Roll the chicken up in the ham and cabbage, like a Swiss roll, using the foil to help you. Roll it as tightly as possible. Wrap the parcel in the foil.

• Place the chicken parcels in an ovenproof dish, and pour in enough stock to come half-way up the parcels. Braise in a pre-heated oven at 180°C (350°F), gas mark 4, for about 25 – 30 minutes or until the chicken feels firm when tested.

• Lift the chicken parcels out and collect all the juices in the dish. Pour into a saucepan and bring to the boil over a moderate heat. Whisk in the remaining butter, cut into small pieces.

• Carve the wrapped chicken into diagonal slices, arrange on the dish and pour the sauce over the top.

Sauté of Sea Bass with Shredded Vegetables

Serves 4

2 fillets of sea bass each weighing about 350 – 450 g (12 oz – 1 lb).
  Ask the fishmonger to fillet the bass for you, but ask for the skin
    to be left on the fillets
seasoned flour
a little sunflower oil
2 carrots, finely sliced
2 leeks, finely sliced
about 125 g (4 oz) celeriac, finely sliced
clove garlic, finely sliced (optional)
1 fresh red chilli, de-seeded and finely sliced (optional)
Japanese naturally brewed soy sauce
lemon juice
water
30 g (1 oz) butter
about 350 g (12 oz) washed young spinach leaves
fresh coriander to garnish

• Cut the sea bass fillets in two to give four portions. On each piece, make four incisions in the skin to prevent the fish curling up during cooking. Coat the skin side only with seasoned flour.

• Heat a small amount of oil in a non-stick frying pan, then place the fish in, skin side down. Cook, without turning, for about four minutes, until the skin is crispy and browned. When the fish is almost cooked through, turn it over and cook for just one more minute on the skinless side.

• While the fish is cooking, heat a little oil in a frying pan or wok. Add the sliced vegetables, and garlic and chilli if desired. Cook quickly over a high heat. Mix together 2 parts of soy sauce to 1 part lemon juice and 1 part water, (for example 4 tablespoons soy sauce, 2 tablespoons lemon juice, 2 tablespoons water). Add the soy mixture to the vegetables together with the butter.

• Heat a little oil in a separate pan and cook the spinach just for a minute, until it just begins to wilt but before any water starts to run out of it.

• Place a bed of spinach in the centre of each plate. Top with the sea bass, skin side up. Spoon the vegetables and sauce around. Garnish with fresh coriander.

Tataki Tuna and Spinach Oshitashi

Serves 4

450 g (1 lb) prepared young spinach leaves
450 g (1 lb) loin of tuna, cut into four
salt
freshly ground black pepper
a little oil
4 tablespoons Japanese naturally brewed soy sauce
juice $^1/_2$ lemon
2 spring onions, thinly sliced
English powder mustard, mixed with a little water
dried bonito flakes (available from oriental stores)

• Cook the spinach in a large pan of vigorously boiling, salted water. Only cook for a few seconds until the spinach collapses, then drain from the water and immediately plunge the spinach into cold water. Squeeze out the excess water and leave the spinach to one side.

• Season the tuna with copious amounts of salt and pepper. Heat a cast iron ridged pan or a heavy based pan until very hot. Lightly oil, then cook the fish for about 30 seconds on each side. The tuna should be seared all around the outside, but still raw in the centre. Immediately plunge the fish into a bowl of iced water and ice cubes, to stop it cooking. Remove from the water and allow to drain.

• Mix together the soy sauce and lemon juice. Add a little water if desired.

• Squeeze the spinach again, then place a little on each plate, spreading it out a little. Pour over the soy sauce. Cut each tuna piece into nine slices and arrange on the plate. Sprinkle the spring onions over the fish and place a teaspoonful of mustard on the side. Finally sprinkle the salad with dried bonito flakes.

Prune and Almond Puff Pastry Tarts

Makes 4

225 g (8 oz) pre-soaked or ready-to-eat stoned prunes.
60 g (2 oz) flaked almonds
60 g (2 oz) plain flour
60 g (2 oz) unsalted butter, at room temperature
1 medium egg
450 g (1 lb) purchased puff pastry
extra flaked almonds to sprinkle
icing sugar for dusting

• To prepare the prunes, put them in hot water and simmer very gently for ten minutes. Drain and leave to become cold. Do not boil the prunes or they may disintegrate.

• To make the frangipane filling, put the almonds, flour and sugar into a food processor and blend well. Add the butter and blend until the mixture is crumbly. Finally, add the egg and blend until the mixture forms a paste.

• Roll out the puff pastry and cut out four 15 cm (6 inch) circles. Place on a baking tray. Divide the frangipane between the four pastry rounds, placing the mixture in little mounds in the centre. It is important to leave a wide rim of uncovered pastry round the edge, as this will allow the pastry to rise and contain the filling. Arrange the prunes on top of the frangipane.

• Feather the edge of the pastry with the back of a small knife, again to help the pastry to rise. Sprinkle over a few flaked almonds and then a little icing sugar.

• Bake in a pre-heated oven at 200 °C (400°F), gas mark 6, for about 20 minutes, until the pastry has risen and is golden brown and the filling has set.

• To finish the tarts, dust with more icing sugar and glaze quickly under a hot grill.

Note – Instead of prunes you may prefer to use apples in this recipe. Simply peel and core a couple of dessert apples, cut into thick slices and soak in a little sugar and lemon juice, then drain.

Hot Chefs

John Tovey

John Tovey worked as a hotel general manager until 1971, when he founded his hotel and restaurant Miller Howe, on the shore of Lake Windermere. He specialises in the best of British cuisine, and his food is required eating for those who believe a list of dishes under that heading would be a few items short of a menu. He has a great admiration for Delia Smith and a great contempt for pretentious cooking. But if you're ever in danger of taking one of these chefs out to dinner, you'd be well advised to stick to Mark Gregory and his $3.50 Chinese meal – John Tovey is more likely to go for caviar and foie gras.

Courgette and Aubergine Savoury Slice

Serves 4

125 g (4 oz) peeled aubergine cut into four thin slices lengthways
a little salt
125 g (4 oz) courgettes, cut into six thin slices lengthways
1 medium egg, lightly beaten
about 2 tablespoons plain flour seasoned with salt and pepper
4 tablespoons sunflower oil

Tomato sauce
2 teaspoons sunflower oil
2 cloves garlic, crushed with a little salt
60 g (2 oz) finely chopped onion
125 g (4 oz) tomato, skinned and chopped

Croutons
4 slices white bread
60 g (2 oz) melted butter

1 whole red pepper
2 tablespoons French dressing

To serve
freshly grated Parmesan cheese.

• Place the aubergine slices on a cooling rack. Lightly sprinkle with salt and leave for a couple of hours for the bitter juice to drain out.

• Dip the aubergine and courgette slices into the beaten egg and then coat in flour. Heat the oil in a frying pan, and when hot fry the slices quickly for about one minute on each side. Drain on kitchen paper.

• To make the tomato sauce, heat the oil in a small pan and add all the other ingredients. Cook gently over a low heat for about ten minutes. You can add one teaspoon of chopped fresh herbs, such as basil, thyme or tarragon, if you like.

• To make the croutons, cut four circles from the bread using a large cutter. Dip the circles in melted butter and place on a baking tray. Bake in the oven at 180°C (350°F), gas mark 4, for about 20 minutes or until crisp and golden brown.

• Cut the red pepper into four segments and remove any pith or seeds. Place each quarter on a board, and make cuts with a small sharp knife to form a fan shape. Put into a steamer and steam for about 15 minutes or until soft. Remove and drain.

• Cut each aubergine slice in two and place one piece on top of the other on a baking ray. Cut each courgette slice in half and arrange three pieces of courgette on top of each aubergine. Put in the oven at 180°C (350°F), gas mark 4, for about 20 minutes to heat through.

• Grill the peppers until they start to turn black. Place a crouton on each of four warmed plates. Top each one with aubergine and courgette. Spoon on a little tomato sauce. Put the fanned pepper to one side and spoon over a little French dressing. Sprinkle with Parmesan cheese and serve at once.

Chicken with Cherries and Almonds

Serves 4

1 free-range chicken, about 1.4 kg/3 lb in weight, cut into ten portions
425 ml (15 fl oz) white wine
seasoned flour
1 tablespoon olive oil
30 g (1 oz) butter, cut in small pieces
2 medium leeks, chopped
1 red pepper, de-seeded and chopped
1 onion, chopped
4 – 6 spring onions, chopped
2 bunches watercress
2 ruby grapefruits, peel and pith removed and segmented
French dressing
450 g (1 lb) stoned morello cherries
60 – 85 g (2 – 3 oz) toasted flaked almonds
2 tablespoons chopped chives

• Put the chicken into an airtight container. Pour over the wine, and leave to marinate in the fridge for up to four days. From time to time, turn the chicken in the marinade.

• Remove the chicken and pat dry. Reserve the marinade. Dust the chicken pieces with seasoned flour. Heat the oil and butter in a small frying pan, and quickly seal the chicken pieces, a few at a time, until golden on all sides.

• Put the leeks, pepper, onion and spring onions into an ovenproof dish. Arrange the chicken pieces on top. Pour over the marinade. Cover and cook in a pre-heated oven at 180°C (350°F), gas mark 4, for about one hour or until the chicken pieces are tender.

• Arrange the watercress around the edge of a large platter. Scatter over the grapefruit segments. Sprinkle with a little French dressing. Place the drained, hot, cooked chicken in the centre. Scatter over the cherries and almonds. Sprinkle with chives and serve.

Turkey Toad-in-the-Hole

Serves 6 – 8

Stock gravy

1.1 litre (2 pints) home-made turkey or chicken stock

Batter

175 g (6 oz) sieved plain flour
2 free-range medium eggs, lightly beaten
175 ml (6 fl oz) cold milk
125 ml (4 fl oz) ice-cold water
salt and freshly ground black pepper
4 tablespoons turkey fat or dripping

Filling

350 g (12 oz) left-over turkey pieces
60 g (2 oz) crushed cornflakes
300 ml (1/2 pint) natural Greek yoghurt
1 medium onion, sliced and lightly fried

• To make the stock gravy put the turkey stock into a pan and simmer gently, uncovered, for three to four hours until it is reduced to 300 ml (1/2 pint). Remove from heat and reserve.

• To make the batter, put the flour into a large bowl and add the eggs, milk, water and seasoning. Using an electric whisk, beat well to form a smooth paste. Leave in a covered bowl in the fridge for two to three hours.

• To make the filling, put the turkey, cornflakes, yoghurt and onion rings into a bowl and mix lightly together.

• Pre-heat the oven to 220°C (425°F), gas mark 7. Put the turkey fat into a large roasting tin and put in the oven for five to ten minutes to heat literally to smoking point. When the fat is very hot, put the roasting tin on the hob switched on low and spread the turkey mixture over the tin. Pour over the batter and return to the oven as quickly as possible.

• Cook in the oven at 220°C (425°F), gas mark 7, for 25 – 30 minutes, until crisp and golden brown. Reheat the stock gravy and serve with the Turkey Toad-in-the-hole.

Lemon Tart

Serves 8 – 12

Farmhouse pastry
175 g (6 oz) self-raising flour
30 g (1 oz) cornflour
175 g (6 oz) softened butter
60 g (2 oz) caster sugar
1 small egg, lightly beaten

Filling
2 unwaxed lemons, cut into eighths and pips removed
350 g (12 oz) sugar, caster or lump sugar
200 ml (7 fl oz) sweet white wine
3 large eggs, lightly beaten

To decorate
300 ml (¹/₂ pint) double cream, whipped together with 2 tablespoons
    sieved icing sugar
lemon slices, cut in quarters
fresh mint leaves

• To make the pastry, sieve the flour and cornflour into a mixing bowl. Add the softened butter in pieces. Rub the butter into the flour. Add the sugar and toss together. Trickle the egg over the mixture and gently mix together to form a soft dough. If it is too soft, wrap in clingfilm and chill for a while in the fridge.

• Roll the dough out to a rough circle and place in a 5 cm (2 inch) deep, 23 cm (9 inch) fluted flan tin. Ease the pastry up the sides of the tin and patch any holes with spare pastry dough.

• Line the flan case with greaseproof or non-stick paper, and fill with baking beans. Bake 'blind' in the oven at 170°C (325°F), gas mark 3, for about 35 minutes. Remove the paper and baking beans for the last few minutes to ensure that the base is thoroughly cooked. Leave the base to cool.

• To make the filling, put the lemons, sugar and wine into a pan. Heat slowly until the sugar has dissolved. Cover and simmer gently, for about 20 minutes, until lemons are tender.

• Pour the lemon, sugar and wine mixture into a food processor or blender. Process for a few seconds until the lemons are thoroughly chopped. Process again and pour in the beaten eggs. Place the cooked flan case, in its tin, on a baking tray. Pour the lemon mixture into the flan case. Bake in the oven at 180°C (350°F), gas mark 4, for about 25 – 30 minutes until filling is set. Cool.

• Remove the cooked flan from the tin and place on a serving dish. Pipe whipped cream round the edge and decorate with lemon slices and fresh mint leaves.

Note – This recipe can be made using oranges instead of lemons.

Sticky Toffee Pudding with Butterscotch Sauce

Serves 8–16

125 g (4 oz) softened butter
175 g (6 oz) soft brown sugar
4 medium eggs, lightly beaten
225 g (8 oz) self-raising flour
1 teaspoon bicarbonate of soda
225 g (8 oz) stoned dates, chopped
2 tablespoons Camp coffee essence
300 ml (10 fl oz) boiling water

Topping
2 tablespoons double cream
85 g (3 oz) soft brown sugar
60 g (2 oz) butter

Butterscotch sauce

225 g (8 oz) golden syrup
60 g (2 oz) softened butter
60 g (2 oz) soft brown sugar
finely grated rind of 2 oranges
few drops of vanilla essence
a little double cream (optional)

• Put all the ingredients except the cream in a small saucepan and stir together over a low heat. If you like, stir in a couple of tablespoons of double cream just before serving.

• Prepare a strong, leak-proof 23 – 25 cm (9 – 10 inch) square cake tin. Line with a double thickness of greaseproof paper and brush with a little melted butter. Place the tin on a baking tray.

• Put the butter and sugar into a bowl and cream well together. Add the beaten eggs a little at a time, mixing well between each addition. Sieve the flour on to this mixture. Fold in gently.

• Put the bicarbonate of soda, dates, and Camp coffee essence into a bowl. Pour over the boiling water. Mix together. Pour the dates and liquid on to the sponge mixture and mix well until you have a smooth runny batter. Pour into the prepared tin.

• Bake in a pre-heated oven at 180°C (350° F), gas mark 4, for about one hour. Just before the pudding is ready, make the topping. To do this, put the ingredients into a small saucepan and bring to the boil. Remove from heat.

• When the pudding is cooked, remove from the oven and pour the topping over it. Brown under a hot grill. Serve the pudding cut into slices with a swirl of whipped cream and accompanied by butterscotch sauce.

Choux Pastry

300 ml (¹/₂ pint) water
125 g (4 oz) soft butter, in small pieces
150 g (5 oz) strong plain flour, sieved
4 eggs, lightly beaten
225 g (8 oz) sieved icing sugar
1 tablespoon Camp coffee essence
a little water
1 teaspoon soft butter
whipped cream

• Pre-heat the oven to 200°C (400°F), gas mark 6. Put the water and butter into a saucepan and gently melt the butter over a low heat.

• Turn up the heat and bring to the boil. Shoot the flour in all at once and beat vigorously with a wooden spoon.

• Put the dough into a bowl. Either use an electric mixer or a bowl with a hand-held mixer, and with the machine on its slowest speed, add the egg a little at a time. The mixture should be shiny and of a strong batter consistency. When all the egg has been added, beat well for one minute.

• Spoon the dough into a piping bag fitted with a large plain nozzle. Use baking trays lined with non-stick silicone paper and sprinkle with cold water. Pipe out éclairs, choux buns or profiteroles according to choice. Smooth the tops or ends with wetted fingers. Put the choux into the oven and immediately turn up the temperature to 220°C (425°F), gas mark 7.

• Choux pastry needs cooking for 10 – 20 minutes according to the size of bun or éclair. Allow to cool.

• To make the coffee icing, put the icing sugar into a bowl and stir in the coffee essence and enough water to give a coating consistency. Beat in the butter. Dip the choux buns into the icing. Fill the buns with whipped cream and serve.

Black Bun with Rum Butter

Serves 12 – 18

Pastry
350 g (12 oz) self-raising flour
125 g (4 oz) cornflour
350 g (12 oz) softened butter
grated rind 1 lemon
125 g (4 oz) caster sugar
2 small eggs, lightly beaten

Filling
350 g (12 oz) raisins
350 g (12 oz) currants
60 g (2 oz) nibbed almonds
60 g (2 oz) crystalised peel, chopped
175 g (6 oz) plain flour, sieved
1 teaspoon ground cinnamon
1 teaspoon ground allspice
1 teaspoon ground nutmeg
generous pinch baking powder
60 g (2 oz) soft light brown sugar
3 tablespoons brandy or malt whisky
4 medium eggs, lightly beaten

Rum Butter

Makes 225 g (8 oz)

125 g (4 oz) softened butter
125 g (4 oz) soft brown sugar
finely grated rind 1 orange
a little finely grated nutmeg
3 tablespoons dark rum

• Cream together the butter and sugar until light and fluffy. Beat in the orange rind and nutmeg. Little by little, beat in the rum. Never add more liquid until the previous measure has disappeared.

• To make the pastry, sieve the flour and cornflour into a mixing bowl. Add the softened butter in pieces. Rub the butter into the flour. Add the lemon rind and sugar and toss together. Trickle the egg over the mixture and gently mix together to form a soft dough. Put in the fridge to chill for a while.

• Break off two thirds of the dough and when it has reached room temperature, roll out and use to line a 5 cm (2 inch) deep, 23 cm (9 inch) fluted flan tin. Push the pastry well up the sides of the tin, and patch any holes with spare dough. Line the flan case with greaseproof or non-stick paper, and fill with baking beans. Bake 'blind' at 170°C (325°F), gas mark 3, for 35 – 40 minutes. Remove the paper and baking beans for the last few minutes to ensure the base is thoroughly cooked. Leave the base to cool.

• To make the filling, put all the dry ingredients into a large bowl and mix well. Add the brandy and eggs and mix well. Spread on the base of the cooked flan case. Take the remaining piece of pastry at room temperature, and roll out to make a lid. Place on top of the pie and press the edges well together.

• Bake in a pre-heated oven at 180°C (350°F), gas mark 4, for one hour. Cover with foil and lower the temperature to 150°C (300°F), gas mark 2, and cook for a further hour. When cold, wrap in foil and store in an air-tight container. Serve with rum butter.

Brown Yoghurt Seed Loaf

Makes two 450 g (1 lb) loaves

60 g (2 oz) self-raising flour
1 teaspoon bicarbonate of soda
$^1/_2$ teaspoon salt
200 g (7 oz) wheatmeal flour
4 heaped tablespoons in all of sunflower, sesame and poppy seeds,
    plus extra sesame seeds for coating
1 egg, lightly beaten
225 ml (8 fl oz) natural yoghurt
3 tablespoons molasses, black treacle or honey
2 teaspoons olive oil, plus extra for greasing

• Pre-heat the oven to 190°C (375°F), gas mark 5, and grease two 450 g (1 lb) loaf tins with oil. Scatter the extra sesame seeds into the tins, allowing them to cover the sides. Line the base with non-stick silicone paper.

• Sieve the self-raising flour, bicarbonate of soda and salt into a bowl. Add the wheatmeal flour and mix well together. Stir in the seeds.

• In a separate bowl, mix together the egg, yoghurt, molasses and oil. Add to the flour mixture and mix together.

• Divide the mixture between the two prepared tins. Smooth the tops level.

• Bake in the oven at 190°C (375°F), gas mark 5, for about 20 – 30 minutes. Test with a sharp knife or skewer to check that the loaves are cooked.

• Leave for ten minutes before turning out of the tins. Allow the loaves to become completely cold before cutting.

Lemon Fork Biscuits

Makes about 18 – 20

225 g (8 oz) soft butter, cut into small pieces
125 g (4 oz) caster sugar
grated rind 1 lemon
275 g (10 oz) sieved plain flour

To decorate
glacé cherries
desiccated coconut
nibbed (chopped) almonds

• Put the butter, sugar, lemon and flour into a bowl. Mix well together until it forms a soft dough. Break off small pieces of dough and roll gently into balls. Place on a baking tray lined with non-stick silicone paper. Space well apart to allow room for the biscuits to spread.

• Dip a large fork in water and press on to each biscuit, flattening it slightly. Decorate with cherries, coconut or almonds according to taste.

• Bake in the oven at 180°C (350°F), gas mark 4, for about 10 – 12 minutes. Allow to cool slightly before transferring to a cooling rack.

Shortbread

Makes about 700 g (1 ¹/₂ lb)

225 g (8 oz) sieved plain flour, plus extra for dusting
125 g (4 oz) farola or fine semolina
125 g (4 oz) caster sugar
225 g (8 oz) soft butter

• Put all the ingredients into a food mixer (not a processor) or use a bowl and a hand-held mixer. Beat on a slow speed until a soft dough is formed.

• Lightly flour the work surface and roll out the shortbread. Using a biscuit cutter of your choice, cut out biscuits and place on a baking tray lined with non-stick silicone paper. Bake in the oven at 180°C (350°F), gas mark 4, for about 10 – 12 minutes.

• Remove from the oven and transfer to a cooling tray. Serve as they are or sandwich together in pairs with jam. Spread the tops with glacé icing and scatter with toasted desiccated coconut.

Strawberry Tartlets

• Make the shortbread as above. Using metal tartlet tins, put a little piece of dough into each one, and press well into the base and up the sides. Trim the edge. Put a cup-cake paper containing baking beans into the shortbread case to stop it rising. Bake in the oven at 180°C (350°F) Gas N° 4 for about 15 minutes.

• Remove the paper and baking beans and gently ease the cooked tartlet cases out of the tins and leave to cool.

• Melt a little plain chocolate and paint the inside of the tartlet with it. Allow to set. To serve, fill with whipped cream and fresh fruit such as strawberries.

Victoria Sponge

Makes three 18 cm (7 in) cakes

225 g (8 oz) unsalted softened butter
225 g (8 oz) caster sugar
4 fresh free-range size 2 eggs, lightly beaten
225 g (8 oz) self-raising flour, sieved

Flavourings
1 teaspoon vanilla essence
1 tablespoon Camp coffee essence
1 tablespoon sieved cocoa powder

Filling
jam and/or whipped cream

To finish
sieved icing sugar

• Put the butter and sugar into a large bowl and cream well together. Add the eggs, a little at a time, beating well between each addition. Gently fold in the flour.

• Divide the mixture between three bowls. Add vanilla essence to one, Camp coffee essence to another and cocoa powder to the last. Mix the flavourings in well. Put each mixture into a greased and base-lined 18 cm (7 inch) sandwich tin. Bake the sponges in a pre-heated oven at 180 °C (350°F), gas mark 4, for about 20 minutes or until firm to the touch. Allow to become cold.

• Slice the cakes in half and spread with jam or whipped cream (or both). Place the tops on and sprinkle liberally with sieved icing sugar.

Note – This amount of Victoria sponge will also make 12 muffins or 24 tiny sponge cakes.

David Wilson

David Wilson became a chef because he loves food – an obvious but none the less vital motive, which fortunately also applies to those who become clients of his restaurant, the Peat Inn, Fife. Clearly a man who knows not only how to butter his bread but on which side his bread is buttered, he says his heroes are Michel Gerard and Patricia Wilson, his wife. His favourite meal is young grouse, simply roasted; his pet hate is an excess of cream in dishes other than puddings.

Ragout of Pork, Scallops and Monkfish in a Spicy Vinaigrette

Serves 4 as a starter

225 g (8 oz) piece of belly pork
chicken stock
1 bay leaf
125 g (4 oz) piece monkfish fillet
8 prepared scallops
a little oil for frying

Vinaigrette
150 ml (5 fl oz) virgin olive oil
50 ml (2 fl oz) white wine vinegar
dark soy sauce
salt and pepper
1 – 2 tablespoons chicken stock

Garnish
2 large tomatoes, blanched, peeled, seeds removed and flesh
    chopped
sprigs of fresh dill

• Cut the pork into small pieces about 1 cm (½ inch) square. Put in a dry pan and quickly stir fry for one to two minutes. Remove and place in a saucepan with the chicken stock, to cover, and a bay leaf. Bring to the boil. Cover and simmer gently for about 45 minutes to an hour, until the pork is very tender. Drain.

• Cut the monkfish into very thin slices. Cut the scallops in half. Spread the pork out on a baking tray and cook under a pre-heated grill until crisp and brown. Heat a little oil in a pan and quickly fry the monkfish slices for one to two minutes each side. Fry the scallop pieces for 30 seconds to one minute each side. Remove and drain.

• To make the warm vinaigrette, put the oil, vinegar, soy sauce, seasoning and chicken stock into a small pan. Heat through very gently; on no account allow the mixture to boil.

• Spoon the pork on to warm serving plates, top with the monkfish and scallops. Spoon the warm vinaigrette on top and around. Garnish with chopped tomato and dill.

Millefeuille of Hazelnut Meringue and Red Fruits

Serves 6

Meringues
8 egg whites
225 g (8 oz) caster sugar
150 g (5 oz) finely ground hazelnuts

Vanilla cream
3 egg yolks
60 g (2 oz) caster sugar
15 g (¹/₂ oz) plain flour
2 teaspoons cornflour
300 ml (¹/₂ pint) milk
¹/₂ vanilla pod, split
300 ml (¹/₂ pint) double cream

Redcurrant purée
225 g (8 oz) redcurrants
125 g (4 oz) caster sugar
1 – 2 tablespoons lemon juice

A selection of red fruits such as strawberries and raspberries

To decorate
icing sugar
fresh redcurrants or raspberries
mint leaves

• To make the meringue, put the egg whites into a bowl and beat until the mixture forms soft peaks. Whisk in half the sugar a little at a time. Then add the remaining sugar and hazelnuts and fold in very gently.

• Fill a piping bag fitted with a large nozzle and pipe out eighteen 7.5 cm (3 inch) circles on trays lined with non-stick silicone paper. Do not make the meringues too thick. Bake in the oven at 100°C (200°F), gas low, for about one to two hours until the meringues are crisp and slightly golden in colour.

• To make the vanilla cream, whisk the egg yolks and sugar together until pale. Sieve the two flours over the egg mixture and stir in. Bring the milk to the boil. Pour on to the egg yolks, whisking well. Sieve back into the pan. Add the vanilla pod and cook gently, stirring continuously until thickened. Cook for two minutes. Remove the vanilla pod and allow custard to cool. Whip the cream until it forms soft peaks and fold it into the cooled custard.

• To make the redcurrant purée, put all ingredients into a food processor and blend. Sieve into a bowl. Taste and add more sugar or lemon juice if desired. Adjust the purée by adding a little water if necessary to give a coating consistency.

• Pour a little redcurrant purée on to each serving dish. Place a meringue in the centre. Spread with vanilla cream and cover with halved strawberries. Place a second meringue on top, spread with vanilla cream and cover with raspberries. Sprinkle the remaining meringue with icing sugar and place on top. Decorate with a few redcurrants or raspberries and fresh mint leaves.

Hot Chefs

Michael Womersley

Given the associations evoked by combining the subjects of food and travel in Britain in the early eighties, the British Transport Hotel, Reading Division, seems an unlikely place for a distinguished chef to have started his career. But so it was with Michael Womersley – at least for about six months. Within ten years he had become head chef at the Lucknam Park Hotel, collected a Michelin star – and met his wife, Jayne, while they were both working at Cliveden, a stately home in Berkshire. Jayne has been a pastry chef for nine years, and has worked at Claridges, and the Inn on the Park.

Truffled Egg with Asparagus

Serves 3 for breakfast

Egg shells
225 g (8 oz) roll or block of cold butter
seasoned flour
beaten egg
fine dried white breadcrumbs
oil for deep frying (preferably peanut or groundnut oil)

Filling
30 g (1 oz) butter
6 eggs
salt and pepper
a little truffle essence (optional)
a little chopped truffle (optional) (you could use chopped chives,
    chopped smoked salmon or grated cheese instead)
225 g (8 oz) fine asparagus, trimmed
toast 'soldiers'

• To make the 'shells', cut the butter into three equal pieces. With a sharp knife, trim into an egg shape. Dip in seasoned flour, coat in beaten egg and then breadcrumbs. Dip again in beaten egg and breadcrumbs and make sure the butter is completely and evenly covered. Chill for a while in the fridge.

• Heat some oil so it is hot enough to brown a piece of day-old bread in a few seconds. Carefully deep fry the coated butter 'eggs' for 10 – 1 5 seconds until golden brown. Remove. Cut off top and drain out the butter. Turn the shell upside down on kitchen paper and allow to dry.

• To make the filling, melt the butter in a pan. Beat the eggs and seasoning well together. Add to the pan and cook, stirring with a wooden spoon, until lightly scrambled. Stir in the truffle essence and truffle.

• Meanwhile cook the asparagus in salted water for about three to five minutes. Drain.

• Put the 'shell' into an egg cup. Fill with scrambled egg. Place lid on top. Serve on a dish with the asparagus and toast 'soldiers'.

Galette of Cornish Crab and Scallops

Serves 2

Galette
2 medium waxy potatoes, peeled and coarsely grated
salt
butter for greasing

1 cooked prepared crab
a little oil for frying

Sauce
¼ onion, chopped
⅓ stick celery, chopped
1 shallot, chopped
½ small leek, chopped
2 button mushrooms, chopped
1 teaspoon chopped parsley
½ bay leaf
½ stalk lemon grass, crushed
1 piece lime zest
½ teaspoon thyme
1 teaspoon tomato purée
1 tablespoon white wine vinegar
1 tablespoon brandy
2 tablespoons chardonnay (or any white wine)
1 tablespoon vermouth
about 150 ml (¼ pint) stock

Filling
2 teaspoons fresh mango, chopped
¼ teaspoon finely chopped fresh root ginger
4 lime segments, chopped
salt and pepper

4 prepared scallops
1 – 2 tablespoons cream
1 teaspoon unsalted butter

To serve
lime segments

- Sprinkle the potato with a little salt and leave for ten minutes. Put in a sieve and rinse well under cold water to remove all the salty liquid. Squeeze very dry with your hands. Liberally butter four 10 cm (4 inch) metal moulds (individual Yorkshire pudding tins work well, or foil dishes). Line the base and sides of two tins with grated potato. In the other two just place potato on the bases, as these will be the 'lids' of the galettes. Cook in a pre-heated oven at 220°C (425°F), gas mark 7, for 20 – 30 minutes until golden brown and crisp. The lids may be ready before the bases.

- Remove the claws from the crab and take out the meat. Remove the meat from the body. Put to one side. Put the crab claw shells into a pan and pound with a rolling pin or meat mallet to break up the shells. Add a little oil to the pan, together with the onion, celery, shallot, leek, mushrooms, parsley, bay leaf, lemon grass, lime zest, thyme and tomato purée. Cook for about ten minutes until the shells are well browned. Add the vinegar, brandy, wine and vermouth and reduce by half. Add just enough stock to cover the shells. Cover and simmer for 20 – 30 minutes.

- Chop the crab meat. Put in a bowl with the mango, ginger and lime segments. Mix well. Fill the galette bases (leaving them in their tins). Put the potato lids on top. Bake in a pre-heated oven at 220°C (425°F), gas mark 7, for five minutes, until heated through.

- Separate the corals from the white part of the scallops. Leave the corals whole, but slice the white flesh. Heat a little oil in a pan, and quickly cook the scallops until golden (about one minute).

- Strain the stock into a clean pan. Heat through. Add seasoning and cream. Whisk in the butter.

- Turn the galettes on to a serving plate. Place the cooked scallops on top and pour the sauce around. Garnish with lime segments.

Salmis of Wood Pigeon with a Parsley and Watercress Sauce

Serves 2

6 wood pigeon breasts
1 clove garlic
1 – 2 tablespoons brandy

Sauce
30 g (1 oz) unsalted butter
2 shallots, finely sliced
4 button mushrooms, finely sliced
1 – 2 tablespoons white wine
1 tablespoon Noilly Prat (optional)
1 bunch washed parsley, about 60 g (2 oz)
1 bunch washed watercress, about 60 g (2 oz)
425 ml (³/₄ pint) chicken stock
salt and pepper
a little cream (optional)

a little olive oil for frying

Garnish
6 baby tomatoes hollowed out and filled with tapenade (ground
    black olives and garlic)
2 carrots, halved, hollowed out and steamed and filled with either
    parsley cream or creamed spinach
(both of the above should be warmed through in the oven)

• Remove the pigeon breasts from the pigeons or ask the butcher to do this for you. Remove the skins from the breasts. Rub each one lightly with a cut clove of garlic. Arrange them in a dish and sprinkle the brandy over them. Leave in a cool place for two hours.

• To make the sauce, heat the butter in a saucepan and gently cook the shallots until transparent but not browned. Add the mushrooms and cook for a minute. Add the wine and Noilly Prat (if desired) and cook for a minute. Add the parsley and watercress and stir until they start to collapse. Pour in the chicken stock. Simmer over a medium heat for 20 – 30 minutes, until parsley and watercress are tender.

• Heat a little olive oil in a frying pan and quickly sauté the pigeon breasts for two to three minutes on each side.

• Put the sauce in a blender or food processor. Process for 15 – 30 seconds. Then sieve into a clean pan. Reheat slowly. Season to taste, add a little cream if desired.

• Pour a little sauce on to each plate. Arrange the pigeon breasts on top. Garnish with the warm carrot boats and tomatoes filled with tapenade.

Chocolate Pudding with Liquorice Sauce and Beaujolais Granita

(Jayne Womersley's recipe)

Serves 6

Granita
85 g (3 oz) caster sugar
85 ml (3 fl oz) water
1 lemon
1 orange
$^{1}/_{2}$ bottle beaujolais

Chocolate puddings
2 whole eggs
2 egg yolks
150 g (5 oz) caster sugar
100 g (3 $^{1}/_{2}$ oz) unsalted butter
85 g (3 oz) extra bitter chocolate
60 g (2 oz) plain flour, sieved

Liquorice sauce
570 ml (1 pint) milk
5 cm (2 inch) approx piece pure liquorice stick, chopped (available in wholefood or health food shops)
about 2.5 – 5 cm (1 – 2 inch) approx piece liquorice root, cut in half (available from wholefood or health food shops)
5 egg yolks
85 g (3 oz) caster sugar
1 – 2 tablespoons double cream

To serve
6 small chocolate cups, either home-made or purchased
fresh mint leaves
icing sugar

• To make the granita, put the sugar and water into a pan and bring to the boil. Stir to dissolve the sugar and remove from heat. Remove the zest from the lemon and orange, cut into strips and blanch. Squeeze the juice from the lemon and orange. Mix together the hot syrup, lemon and orange zests and juice and the wine. Leave to infuse for 15 – 20 minutes. Strain into a suitable container and freeze for at least six hours.

• To make the puddings, put the eggs, egg yolks and sugar into a bowl and whisk until pale. In a bowl over a pan of hot water, melt the butter and chocolate together. When the chocolate is melted and hot, whisk well into the egg mixture. Fold in the sieved flour. Butter six 7$^{1}/_{2}$ x 4 cm (3 x 1$^{1}/_{2}$ inch) ramekins. Line the bases with circles of greaseproof paper. Pour the mixture into the dishes and bake in a pre-heated oven at 180°C (350°F), gas mark 4, for 12 – 15 minutes.

• To make the sauce, bring the milk to the boil. Add the liquorice stick and root and re-boil the milk to infuse the flavours. Stir well. Whisk the egg yolks and sugar together until pale. Pour the milk through a sieve, on to the eggs, whisking continuously. Strain this mixture back into the pan and stir slowly over a gentle heat until it just coats the back of a spoon. Remove from heat and stir in the cream.

• Remove the granita from the freezer and fork into coarse crystals. Spoon a little granita into each chocolate cup and decorate with mint leaves.

• Turn the chocolate puddings out on to serving plates. Place a chocolate cup to one side. Pour some liquorice sauce around the puddings and sprinkle with a little icing sugar.

Note – When cut open the puddings should have a chocolate sauce in the centre.